THE
CHIHUAHUA

by Charlotte Wilcox

Consultant:
Sandra Whittle, President
Chihuahua Club of America

C A P S T O N E
H IGH/ L OW B OOKS
an imprint of Capstone Press
Mankato, Minnesota

Capstone High/Low Books are published by Capstone Press
818 North Willow Street, Mankato, Minnesota 56001
http://www.capstone-press.com

Library of Congress Cataloging-in-Publication Data
Wilcox, Charlotte.
    The Chihuahua/by Charlotte Wilcox.
    p. cm.—(Learning about dogs)
    Includes bibliographical references (p. 44) and index.
    Summary: An introduction to the smallest of all dog breeds, covering its
history, development, habits, and required care.
    ISBN 0-7368-0158-8
    1. Chihuahua dogs—Juvenile literature. [1. Chihuahua. (Dog breed.) 2. Dogs.]
I. Title II. Series: Wilcox, Charlotte. Learning about dogs.
SF429.C45W55   1999
636.76—dc21   98-37633
                                                                                CIP
                                                                                 AC

Editorial Credits

Timothy Halldin, cover designer; Kimberly Danger and Sheri Gosewisch,
    photo researchers

*(The affiliation of the consultant with the Chihuahua Club of America does not
indicate the endorsement of this book by the Chihuahua Club of America.)*

Photo Credits

Cheryl A. Ertelt, 26, 30, 33, 37, 38–39
Faith Uridel, cover
Kent and Donna Dannen, 4, 18, 22, 28
Oscar C. Williams, 20
Photobank, Inc./Eva Marie Hanlon, 34
Photri/Lani, 13
Unicorn Stock Photos/D & I MacDonald, 43
Uniphoto/Wolfgang Freithof, 10; Rick Brady, 46
Yahweh Chihuahuas/Cynda Seibert, 6, 9, 14, 16, 25

Table of Contents

Quick Facts about the Chihuahua

Description

Height: Chihuahuas stand 6 to 9 inches (15 to 23 centimeters) tall. Height is measured from the ground to the withers. The withers are the tops of the shoulders.

Weight: Most Chihuahuas weigh 2 to 6 pounds (1 to 3 kilograms). They can weigh as much as 10 pounds (4.5 kilograms).

Physical features: Chihuahuas are the smallest of all dog breeds. They have large, round eyes. Their large ears stand straight out from their heads. The Chihuahua's head has a high, rounded top. They can have either short or long hair.

Colors: Chihuahuas can be black, gray, white, brown, or tan. Some have tan or white patches. Others have streaks or markings of black or brown.

Development

Place of origin: The first Chihuahuas came from Mexico.

History of breed: Chihuahuas came from early dogs of southern North America. They may have been crossbred with dogs from Asia.

Numbers: The American Kennel Club registers about 35,000 Chihuahuas each year. The Canadian Kennel Club registers about 500 Chihuahuas each year. To register means to record a dog's breeding record with an official club.

Uses

Chihuahuas make good family pets.

Chapter 1
The World's Smallest Dog

Chihuahuas (chuh-WAH-wahz) are the smallest dogs in the world. Most Chihuahuas weigh 2 to 6 pounds (1 to 3 kilograms). A Chihuahua can fit in the pouch of a backpack.

Chihuahuas do not take up much room. They make good pets for people in apartments. They do not need a big yard.

Chihuahuas are easy to care for. Their small size makes them easy to handle. They can ride

A Chihuahua can fit in the pouch of a backpack.

easily in small cars. Some people even carry their Chihuahuas in baskets on their bicycles.

Most Chihuahuas get along well with people. Chihuahuas seem to like to be petted. They are easy to hold because they are so small. Chihuahuas are lively and can be fun to train.

A Toy Breed

The Chihuahua breed is called a toy breed. Toy breeds are dog breeds that are very small. Some toy breeds are small versions of larger breeds. For example, toy poodles look just like standard poodles. But they are much smaller. A poodle is a breed of dog with thick, curly hair.

Chihuahuas are not a small version of another breed. They do not look like any other dog. They are a breed all their own.

Chihuahuas are lively and can be fun to train.

Chapter 2
The Beginnings of the Breed

Chihuahuas are named after Chihuahua, Mexico. The state of Chihuahua is near the United States border. It is close to Texas and New Mexico. In the 1800s, travelers from the United States discovered Chihuahuas in Mexico.

No one knows the true origin of the Chihuahua. There are many opinions and ideas about the first Chihuahuas.

Some people think Chihuahuas first came from Egypt. Remains of tiny dogs that look like

Opinions and ideas vary about where the first Chihuahuas came from.

Chihuahuas were found in Egypt. These remains were about 3,000 years old. But no one knows how Egyptian dogs may have reached Mexico.

Other people think Chihuahuas came from China. Trading ships may have brought these dogs to Mexico. These ships would have arrived in the 1700s or 1800s.

A North American Breed

Most people think Chihuahuas are native to North America. The Toltec (TOHL-tek) people carved pictures of tiny dogs into stones in Mexico. The Toltecs carved the pictures about 1,000 years ago. These dogs look much like the Chihuahuas of today.

The Toltecs called their little dogs Techichi (teh-CHEE-chee). The Techichi were a bit larger than modern Chihuahuas. Their colors were similar to the colors of today's Chihuahuas.

The Techichi did not do work for people like many other dogs did. They were too

Chihuahuas may be native to Mexico. They sometimes appear in Mexican art.

small to herd livestock or hunt game. They could not carry packs or pull loads.

The Toltecs highly valued the Techichi. Toltecs believed that the friendship between humans and dogs continued after death. They believed that the Techichi led them into life after death. A Techichi often was killed after its Toltec owner died. The Techichi was buried with its owner. Techichi remains have been found in human graves.

The Toltecs ruled central Mexico from about A.D. 900 to 1150. Then crop failures and new migrations to central Mexico ended their power there.

The Chihuahua is too small to do work for people.

Chapter 3
The Development of the Breed

People from Europe came to Mexico in the early 1500s. They found some of the stones with the Techichi pictures carved on them. Europeans built a church with the stones. This church still stands near Mexico City. Visitors still can see the pictures of little dogs on the stones.

Europeans brought the Christian religion to Mexico. Many Mexicans became Christians. Christians are people who follow the teachings of Jesus Christ. The people then no longer

Today, the tiny Chihuahua is a popular pet.

Chihuahuas came to the United States around 1850. Owners began to show them at dog shows in the late 1800s.

believed they needed dogs to guide them after death. The little dogs became less important. Fewer people raised Techichis.

Techichis became smaller and smaller over time. They may have been crossbred with smaller Mexican dogs. To crossbreed means to mate two different types of dogs. Some people think these smaller dogs first came from Asia.

Discovered Again

Travelers from the United States first saw the tiny dogs from Mexico around 1850. The travelers were touring the state of Chihuahua, Mexico. They visited the remains of an ancient palace. Some tiny dogs ran out to meet them.

The travelers had never seen such small dogs. They named the little dogs Chihuahuas. They brought some Chihuahuas back to the United States.

The tiny dogs made excellent pets. People in North America began to breed and raise them. Owners began to show Chihuahuas at dog shows in the late 1800s.

The American Kennel Club registered the first Chihuahua in 1904. To register means to record a dog's breeding record with an official club. Today, the American Kennel Club registers about 35,000 Chihuahuas each year. The Canadian Kennel Club registers about 500 Chihuahuas each year.

Chapter 4
The Chihuahua Today

Today, Chihuahuas are popular pets in North America. Owners enjoy having these small, lively dogs as part of their families.

Most Chihuahuas have long tails. The tails can be fluffy or smooth. Some Chihuahuas are born with a short tail called a bobtail. Dog clubs do not allow Chihuahuas with bobtails to be in dog shows.

Chihuahuas' eyes are large and round. Some people think this makes even adult Chihuahuas look like puppies. Most Chihuahuas have dark eyes. Some lighter-colored Chihuahuas have light eyes.

Chihuahuas are easy to carry and care for.

Chihuahuas' heads have a high, rounded shape. This shape is called an apple dome. Chihuahuas have ears that stick out from the sides of their heads. Most other dog breeds do not have ears like these. Chihuahuas' ears stand up straight when the dogs are alert. The ears stand out to the sides when these dogs are relaxed.

A Hole in the Head

Puppies of all breeds are born with a hole in the front of their skulls. This makes the head soft so the puppy can have an easier birth. The hole cannot be seen because it is in the bone. It is covered with skin and hair. The bone usually grows together as the puppy grows up.

In some Chihuahuas, the bone never grows together. This does not mean the Chihuahua is sick. Chihuahuas still live long, healthy lives with this hole in their skull.

The ears of Chihuahuas stand up straight when the dogs are alert.

Sizes of Chihuahuas

Chihuahuas are the tiniest dog breed. They weigh only 3 to 6 ounces (85 to 170 grams) at birth. That is less than an apple or an orange. Two newborn Chihuahuas together would weigh about as much as this book.

Full-grown Chihuahuas usually weigh 2 to 6 pounds (1 to 3 kilograms). Some can weigh much more. Dog clubs do not allow Chihuahuas that weigh more than 6 pounds (3 kilograms) to be in dog shows.

Adult Chihuahuas stand 6 to 9 inches (15 to 23 centimeters) tall. The height is measured from the ground to the withers. The withers are the tops of the shoulders.

Different Coats

A dog's hair is called its coat. Chihuahuas can have either long coats or smooth coats. Those with smooth coats have hair that is shorter than their long-coat relatives. Some Chihuahuas have thicker coats than others. Chihuahuas with different coat types can look very different from one another.

Chihuahuas can have long coats or smooth coats.

Long-coated Chihuahuas have long, soft hair. It can be straight or a little curly. Extra hair grows on their ears, tails, legs, and necks.

Smooth-coated Chihuahuas have short, smooth hair. The hair on their ears, necks, and stomachs is thin.

Chihuahuas keep themselves very clean. Sometimes Chihuahuas lick their paws and wash their faces like cats do. Their coats are easy to keep neat and clean. This helps make them good pets.

Chihuahua Colors

Chihuahuas can be many colors. They can be black, brown, gray, white, or tan. Chihuahuas' coats can be solid, splashed, or marked. Solid coats are all one color. Splashed coats have patches of a color on a white background.

Marked Chihuahuas can be many styles. Some are mostly solid with a few white or tan markings. The markings usually are on the face, chest, stomach, legs, or tail.

Chihuahuas can be black, brown, gray, white, or tan. Their coats can be solid, splashed, or marked.

Other marking styles include sable and brindle. Sable means some tan hairs are black or brown on the ends. Brindle means the tan hairs are streaked with black or brown hairs. This creates a striped appearance. Sable and brindle markings appear most often in tan or brown Chihuahuas. These markings are not rare. But they are not seen as often as some other markings.

Marked Chihuahuas usually have markings on the face, chest, stomach, legs, or tail.

Chapter 5
Owning a Chihuahua

Chihuahuas can make good pets for many people. People who cannot keep large dogs can enjoy Chihuahuas. Chihuahuas do well in city apartments or homes with small yards. They usually get along with most people, including children.

Chihuahuas do not always get along well with other dogs. Chihuahuas seem to recognize their own breed. They usually are friendly to other Chihuahuas. But they often are not friendly to other dog breeds.

Chihuahuas usually get along with most people, including children.

Finding a Chihuahua

The best way to find a Chihuahua is through a breeder. Breeders can be found by calling a dog club. There are 20 Chihuahua clubs in the United States. The Chihuahua Club of America has the names and locations of these clubs. Breeders usually do not sell their dogs in pet stores. Pet stores may sell dogs that are not healthy. These dogs also may not get along well with people or other dogs.

There are other places to find Chihuahuas. People may look for Chihuahuas at dog shows. Dog trainers also may know of pets for sale. Veterinarians may have names of good Chihuahua breeders. A veterinarian is a person trained to treat sick or injured animals.

Sometimes Chihuahuas can be adopted. Breed clubs or rescue shelters may know of these dogs. Rescue shelters find homes for homeless dogs. To adopt a dog usually costs less than to buy one from a breeder. Some adopted dogs are free. They may even be trained.

The best way to find a Chihuahua is through the Chihuahua Club of America.

Chihuahuas become cold easily and must be kept warm.

Caring for a Chihuahua

Most Chihuahuas are healthy and strong. They generally live to be 12 to 15 years old. This is longer than many other breeds. Some Chihuahuas have reached 20 years of age.

Chihuahuas are easier to care for than some other breeds. They are easy to control and clean up after. Their beds, toys, and dishes take up little room. They do not create as much waste as other dogs.

Chihuahuas do have some special needs. Chihuahuas must be kept warm. They become cold easily, even in warm locations. Many Chihuahua owners provide little sweaters or jackets for their dogs. Chihuahuas often shiver. This can be from excitement or from cold. Chihuahuas should always sleep indoors.

Chihuahuas need exercise. They are easy for most people to take for walks. Chihuahuas do not run as fast as large breeds. They do not pull as hard on leashes.

Chihuahuas should never be left outside alone. They must be on leashes or inside fences at all times. Chihuahuas should be protected from other dogs and wild animals. Coyotes, owls, and other dogs can kill Chihuahuas. Other animals such as skunks and raccoons also can harm them.

Feeding a Chihuahua

Chihuahuas do not need much food. Most owners feed Chihuahuas dry dog food. Adult Chihuahuas may eat 2 to 3 ounces (57 to 85 grams) of dry food each day. Dry dog food is good for Chihuahuas' teeth and keeps their gums healthy. Many owners keep dry food out all day for puppies. That way, puppies can eat whenever they get hungry. Puppies' stomachs are too little to store up food for a long time.

Many Chihuahua owners prepare homemade food for their dogs. Chihuahuas can eat meats such as chicken, turkey, or beef. They can eat snacks such as raw vegetables and fruits. Chewing raw bones helps keep Chihuahuas' teeth clean. Cooked bones are not good for dogs.

Most people feed their Chihuahuas two or three small meals a day. It is important not to feed dogs more than they need. Chihuahuas that eat too much can become overweight. This can lead to health problems.

Chihuahuas need plenty of fresh water each day. They should be able to drink whenever they want. Chihuahuas should drink at least three times a day.

Grooming

Chihuahuas need to be groomed. They must be kept neat and clean. Chihuahuas' coats should

Chihuahuas generally live to be 12 to 15 years old.

be combed or brushed regularly. Chihuahuas' toenails often grow too long. They must be clipped regularly. Chihuahuas should have a bath about once a month.

Chihuahuas need their teeth brushed once a week. This is important so dogs do not get sick. Owners can buy special toothpaste for dogs. Dogs should never have human toothpaste. It is made to be spit out. Dogs cannot spit. They need toothpaste they can swallow.

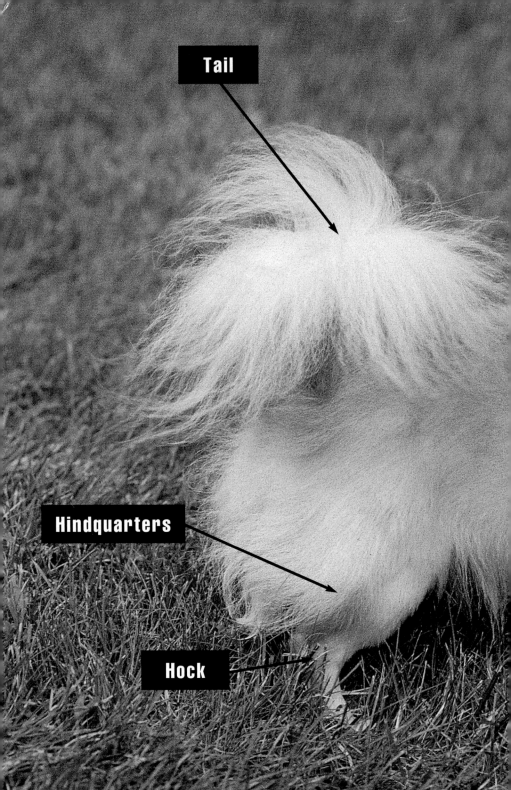

Tail

Hindquarters

Hock

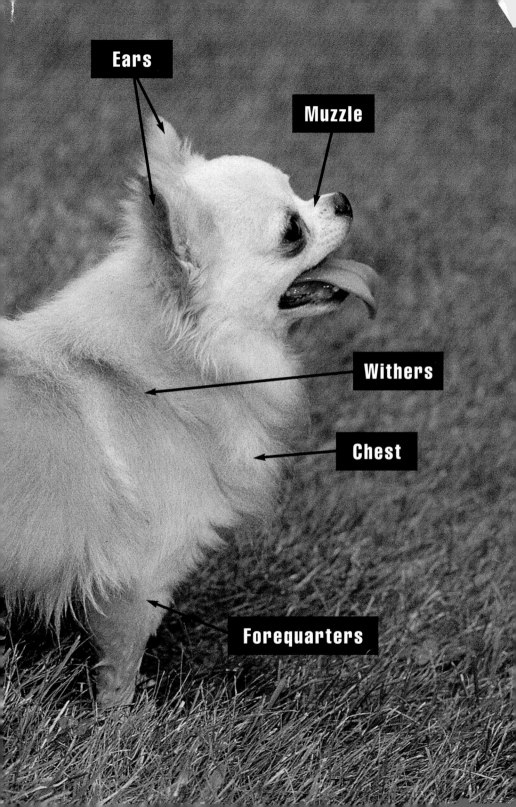

Ears

Muzzle

Withers

Chest

Forequarters

Quick Facts about Dogs

Dog Terms

A male dog is called a dog. A female dog is called a bitch. A young dog is called a puppy until it is 1 year old. A newborn puppy is called a whelp until it no longer needs its mother's milk. A family of puppies born at one time is called a litter.

Life History

Origin: All dogs, wolves, coyotes, and dingoes descended from a single wolf-like species. Humans trained dogs throughout history.

Types: There are about 350 official dog breeds in the world. Dogs come in different sizes and colors. Adult dogs weigh from 2 pounds (1 kilogram) to more than 200 pounds (91 kilograms). They range from 6 inches (15 centimeters) to 36 inches (91 centimeters) tall.

Reproductive life: Dogs mature at 6 to 18 months. Puppies are born two months after breeding. A female can have two litters per year. An average litter has three to six puppies. Litters of 15 or more puppies are possible.

Development: Newborn puppies cannot see or hear. Their ears and eyes open one to two weeks after birth. Puppies try to walk when they are 2 weeks old. Their teeth begin to come in when they are about 3 weeks old.

Life span: Dogs are fully grown at 2 years. They can live 15 years or longer with good care.

The Dog's Super Senses

Smell: Dogs have a strong sense of smell. It is many times stronger than a human's. Dogs use their noses more than their eyes and ears. They recognize people, animals, and objects just by smelling them. They may recognize smells from long distances. They also may remember smells for long periods of time.

Hearing: Dogs hear better than people do. Dogs can hear noises from long distances. They also can hear high-pitched sounds that people cannot hear.

Sight: Dogs' eyes are farther to the sides of their heads than people's are. They can see twice as wide around their heads as people can.

Touch: Dogs enjoy being petted more than almost any other animal. They also can feel vibrations from approaching trains or the beginnings of earthquakes or storms.

Taste: Dogs do not have a strong sense of taste. This is partly because their sense of smell overpowers their sense of taste. It also is partly because they swallow food too quickly to taste it well.

Navigation: Dogs often can find their way home through crowded streets or across miles of wilderness without guidance. This is a special ability that scientists do not fully understand.

Words to Know

bobtail (BOB-tayl)—a short tail; some bobtails are natural and others are made by cutting off the tail.

brindle (BRIN-duhl)—tan hairs streaked with black or brown

coat (KOHT)—an animal's hair

groom (GROOM)—to keep an animal neat and clean

register (REJ-uh-stur)—to record a dog's breeding record with an official club

sable (SAY-buhl)—tan hairs with black or brown ends

veterinarian (vet-ur-uh-NER-ee-uhn)—a person trained to treat sick or injured animals

withers (WITH-urs)—the tops of an animal's shoulders; a dog's height is measured from the ground to the withers.

To Learn More

American Kennel Club. *The Complete Dog Book for Kids.* New York: Howell Book House, 1996.

Driscoll, Laura. *All About Dogs and Puppies.* All Aboard Books. New York: Grosset & Dunlap, 1998.

Hansen, Ann Larkin. *Dogs.* Popular Pet Care. Minneapolis: Abdo & Daughters, 1997.

Rosen, Michael J. *Kids' Best Dog Book.* New York: Workman, 1993.

You can read articles about Chihuahuas in *AKC Gazette*, *Dog Fancy*, *Dogs in Canada*, and *Dog World* magazines.

Useful Addresses

American Kennel Club
5580 Centerview Drive
Raleigh, NC 27606

Canadian Kennel Club
89 Skyway Avenue, Suite 100
Etobicoke, ON M9W 6R4
Canada

Chihuahua Club of America
16 Hillgirt Road
Hendersonville, NC 28792

Chihuahua Club of Canada
2114 Dublin Street
New Westminster, BC V3M 3A9
Canada

Internet Sites

American Kennel Club
http://www.akc.org

Canadian Kennel Club
http://www.ckc.ca

Dogs in Canada
http://www.dogs-in-canada.com

Pet Net
http://www.petnet.com

Index